AUG 1 9 2011

Cecil County Public Library
301 Newark Ave.
Elkton, MD 21921

D1789040

Chimpanzees

by Dan Greenberg with Christina Wilsdon

New York

Marshall Cavendish Benchmark
99 White Plains Road
Tarrytown, NY 10591
www.marshallcavendish.us

Text copyright © 2010 by Marshall Cavendish Corporation

All rights reserved. No part of this book may be reproduced or utilized in any form or by any means electronic or mechanical, including photocopying, recording, or by any information storage and retrieval system, without permission from the copyright holders.

All websites were available and accurate when this book was sent to press.

Library of Congress Cataloging-in-Publication Data

Greenberg, Daniel A.
   Chimpanzees / by Dan Greenberg, with Christina Wilsdon.
     p. cm. – (Benchmark rockets. Animals)
   Includes bibliographical references and index.
   Summary: "Describes the physical characteristics, habitat, behavior, diet, life cycle, and conservation status of chimpanzees"–Provided by publisher.
     ISBN 978-0-7614-4341-4 (alk. paper)
1. Chimpanzees–Juvenile literature. I. Wilsdon, Christina. II. Title.

QL737.P96G7533 2010
599.885–dc22
2008052102

Publisher: Michelle Bisson
Editorial Development and Book Design: Trillium Publishing, Inc.

Photo research by Trillium Publishing, Inc.

Cover photo: Shutterstock.com/Kitch Bain

The photographs and illustrations in this book are used by permission and through the courtesy of: *iStockphoto.com*: Windzepher, 1; Chanyut Sribua-rawd, 4–5; Jeryl Tan, 9, 14; Editorial12, 10–11; Gary Wales, 16–17. *Marshall Cavendish Benchmark*: 6, 12. *Shutterstock.com*: Norma Cornes, 8; Xavier Marchant, 13; Ronald van der Bee, 19. *Sunny Gagliano*: 18. *AP Photo*: Jean-Marc Bouju, 20. *Chimpanzee and Human Communication Institute, https://www.cwu.edu/~cwuchci*: 21.

Printed in Malaysia
1 3 5 6 4 2

Contents

1. What Is a Chimpanzee? 5
2. Chimpanzee Life 11
3. The Future of Chimpanzees 17

   Glossary 22

   Find Out More 23

   Index 24

A chimp's arms and legs help it climb.

Chapter 1
What Is a Chimpanzee?

Lucy was thirsty. She opened the refrigerator and got a cold drink. Then she sat in a chair to look at a magazine. She found a picture of a poodle. "That dog!" Lucy said, in sign language.

What Lucy did seems normal, until you find out that Lucy isn't a person. She's a chimpanzee!

Chimpanzees are more like people than any other animal. They do things people do. They hug each other. They laugh, play, and tickle each other. They show off and act silly. They smile, frown, and cry.

Chimpanzees

Chimpanzees are often called *chimps*. Chimps and people are part of a group of animals called **primates**. Monkeys and gorillas are in this group, too.

Chimps and people are alike in many ways. However, our bodies and their bodies are quite different.

A chimp's body helps it live and move in the forest. Its arms are long. This helps it climb trees and swing from branches.

A chimp has four fingers and a thumb on each hand, like people do. But a chimp's fingers are long and curved. This makes it easy for a chimp to hook its fingers over a branch and hang.

A chimp's foot looks different from a person's foot. It looks more like a person's hand. The big toe points away from the other toes, the same way a person's thumb points away from the

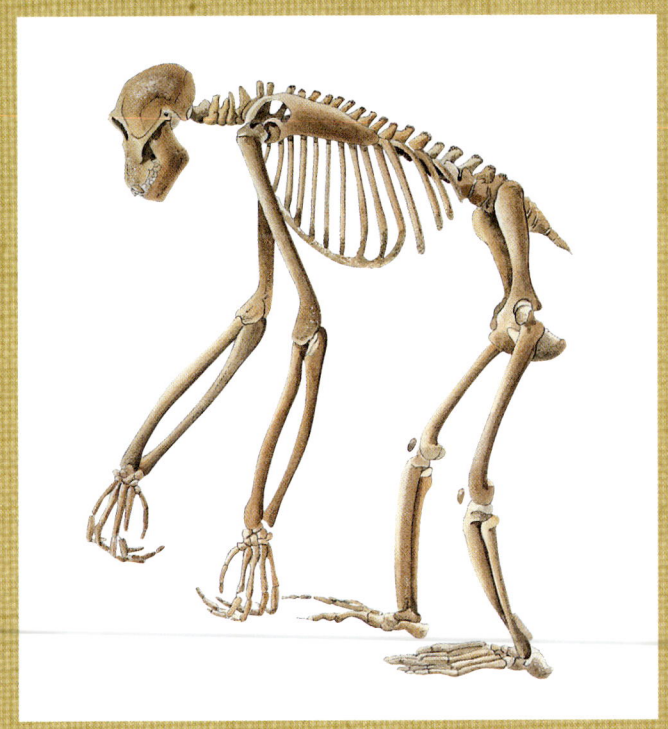

A chimp has long arms and long, curved legs. Chimps can stand up straight but usually walk on all fours.

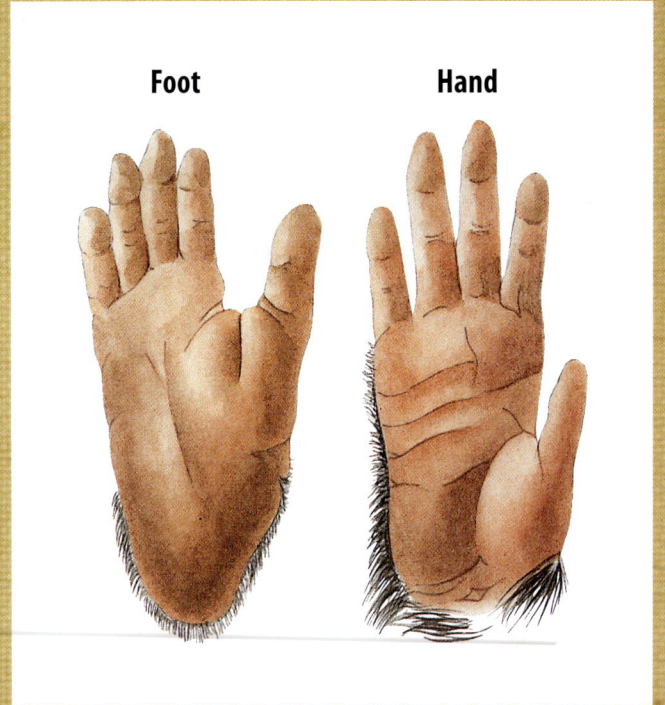

A chimp's toes work like fingers. This helps the chimp climb and carry things.

other fingers. A chimp's big toe works like a person's thumb, too. A chimp uses it to hold onto branches and to carry things. Yes, chimps can carry things with their feet!

Chimps are three times as strong as most people. They are shorter than most people, even when they stand up tall. Chimps' backs and legs curve in a different

CHIMPANZEES

way than people's do. This means chimps can't stand up for very long. Most of the time they use their arms and legs to walk. When they do this, they lean on the back of their fingers.

Chimps have large brains. Their brains are smaller than people's brains, but chimps are still very smart. And they learn quickly.

Most animals are not smart enough to make tools. But chimps make and use tools to get food and water.

This chimp uses a stick to pull bugs out from underground, where they live.

Termites are one thing chimps like to eat. Chimps make tools to help them catch termites. First, they get a stick and pull off any leaves. Then they push the stick into a

What Is a Chimpanzee?

termite hole. The termites get angry and grab the stick with their jaws. Quickly, the chimps pull out the stick and eat the termites. Chimps also use sticks to get honey out of bees' nests.

Chimps use other tools, too. Some chimps use rocks as tools. They break open nuts with them. Chimps even make sponges. They chew up leaves to make the leaves soft. Then they put the leaves into a puddle of water. The leaves soak up the water. Then the chimps suck out the water from the leaves.

Being smart helps chimps get along in groups, where they need to **communicate** with other chimps. They must remember who's who—and who's the boss!

Baby chimps learn from grown-ups.

Chimps spend most of their time in groups.

Chapter 2
Chimpanzee Life

Chimps live in a group called a **community**. A small community may have only 15 chimps. Big communities may have up to one hundred.

Each community has one leader. The leader is a male who is very loud and fierce. All of the chimps in the community follow his rules. Young males stay out of his way.

A chimp becomes a leader by making other males afraid of him. Sometimes he fights to show off his strength. Sometimes he just acts scary. He will slap the ground and scream to make others afraid. He will show his teeth and throw sticks.

Chimpanzees

Every chimp in a community knows where he or she fits within the group. This place is called its **rank**. Chimps with a low rank are careful to show respect to chimps with a higher rank.

During the day, the chimps in a community break up into small groups. Some males do not go with a group. Instead, they spend the day alone. Chimps spend most of the day looking for food. They eat fruit, nuts, seeds, flowers, and leaves. They also eat eggs and bugs. When chimps find food, they call to the other chimps. They grunt and make loud sounds.

Sometimes, chimps catch and eat monkeys, bats, or **bushpigs**. Chimps are very noisy when they catch something. Other chimps hear their loud sounds and come running. They want to join the feast.

A chimp with a low rank bows down to a chimp with a high rank. While he bows, the chimp grunts to say, "You're the boss."

CHIMPANZEE LIFE

Chimps also spend a lot of the day **grooming** each other. They pick dirt, **ticks**, and other bugs out of each other's fur. Mothers groom babies and young chimps. Grown-ups take turns grooming each other.

Grooming keeps chimps clean. It also helps keep their community strong. Grooming helps chimps feel safe and calm. After two chimps fight, they may sit down and groom each other. Grooming helps them become friends again.

At the end of the day, all of the chimps meet up again. They come together at night to sleep in trees. There they are safe from animals that hunt them, such as leopards. Each chimp makes a nest of leaves and branches. A chimp makes a new nest every night.

Grooming is important for chimps of all ages.

Female chimps become mothers when they are about 13 years old. They start looking for a mate about one year before that time. Most females will have a baby every five years or so.

A mother chimp stays close to her baby almost all the time. A mother chimp and her baby spend years together. They are together longer than most animal families are. This is another way that chimps are like people.

A mother chimp hugs and carries her baby. She plays with it, too. As it gets older, the baby also plays with other baby chimps. If it cries out, its mother hurries over to protect it. When a chimp is five years old, its mother may

Mother's Helpers

When a baby is born, other females from the community help the mother. They comfort her during birth. They help clean the new baby. The whole chimp community gets excited about the new baby. Grown-ups go out of their way to play with the baby.

The Life of a Chimp

Years

- **0** — A baby chimp stays near its mother. She keeps it safe. It learns from her.
- **5** — A chimp may become a big brother or sister.
- **10** — Female chimps are ready to have babies.
- **15–20** — When a male is old enough, he challenges the community's leader. If he wins, he becomes the leader. If he loses, he leaves the community.
- **25–35** — Female chimps may have a baby every five years, until they are 35 years old.
- **40** — Chimps in the wild often live to be 40. Chimps in zoos can live even longer.

Chimpanzee Life

have a new baby. Even then, the young chimp will stay with its mother.

A young chimp learns by watching its mother. It sees how she finds food. It eats the food its mother eats. It watches how she acts with other chimps. Then it copies her.

Young male chimps learn not to make other male chimps angry. But as they get older, they start bossing around other males. Each young male wants to be the leader of the community one day. Each one wants to show that he can be fierce and loud.

Chimps find food and safety in forests.

Chapter 3
The Future of Chimpanzees

All chimps live in forests. Forests give chimps food and keep them safe. Many chimps live in rain forests. These thick, green forests are warm and wet all year.

Chimps can live in other kinds of forests, too. This is because chimps are smart and can get used to new places. They learn where to find food. They even try new foods.

Some chimps live in forests high up on mountains. Other chimps live in small forests on wide, grassy lands.

Chimpanzees

When people cut or burn down forests, chimps can lose their home. Today, there are fewer places for chimps to live than ever before. There are also a lot fewer chimps. More than one million chimps lived in Africa about one hundred years ago. Now, there may be only 150,000 wild chimps. That is less than the number of people born each day. Chimps have become **endangered**. If things stay the same, they will die out.

Cutting and burning down forests is not the only thing that hurts chimps. Pollution and people do, too. Some people hunt chimps for meat. Others catch chimps and sell them as pets, to be used in shows, or for science.

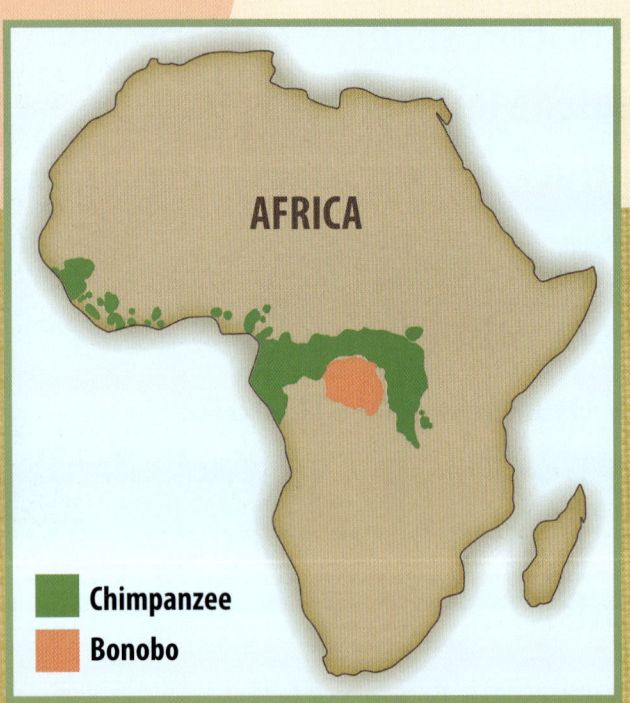

Chimps live in forests in parts of Africa. A close relative of the chimp called the bonobo lives in African forests, too.

The Future of Chimpanzees

Can chimps be helped? Many people think so. Around the world, people are working hard to help chimps. Many countries have passed laws to protect chimps. Many scientists have stopped taking chimps from the wild. Some countries in Africa have set up big parks. These parks help keep chimps safe and protect the forests, too.

Scientists are busy learning a lot about chimps in the wild. Their work helps save chimps. This is because people find out about what scientists have learned. They become interested in chimps and want to help them. It is sad for people to think about a world without chimps.

Chimps and Bonobos

Bonobos are a lot like chimps. They are sometimes called *pygmy chimpanzees*.

It's easy to tell a bonobo from a chimp. A bonobo is thinner than a chimp. The hair on its head parts down the middle. A chimp's hair does not. Bonobos are more peaceful than chimps. Also, female bonobos have more power in their communities than female chimps do.

Like chimps, bonobos are endangered. There may be only 13,000 wild bonobos left.

Chimpanzees

Dr. Jane Goodall spent many years getting to know chimps in their homes.

A lot of what we know about chimps comes from one scientist. Her name is Dr. Jane Goodall. In 1960, Goodall went to Africa to study chimps in the wild. She was the first scientist to see chimps make and use tools. She learned that chimps hunt other animals and eat meat. She learned that chimp communities sometimes fight with other chimp communities. She also saw how chimps communicate with each other.

Since learning about Goodall's work, other scientists have gone to study chimps in the wild. A few years ago, scientists saw chimps that hunted with spears. The chimps bit sticks to make them sharp. Then they stuck the sharp sticks into tree holes. They caught small primates called bush babies with their spears.

The Future of Chimpanzees

Some scientists have worked with chimps in labs. They have taught chimps to use sign language. Both chimps and people can learn sign language. They can use this language to communicate with each other.

Washoe learned sign language from Roger and Deborah Fouts. The Foutses teach at a college in Washington State.

One chimp learned 132 signs. Her name was Washoe. She could make sentences, and she could answer questions. Washoe's son learned to make signs, too. He copied his mother, like baby chimps do!

But chimps do not need to learn sign language to tell us they need help. We know that chimps need us to help save the forests they live in. It is up to us to protect these animals that are so much like us.

Glossary

bushpigs: Small hairy pigs that live in some forests in Africa.

communicate: To share information, ideas, and feelings in a way that others can understand.

community: A group of people or chimpanzees that know each other, follow the same rules, and live in one place.

endangered: In danger of dying out.

grooming: Cleaning an animal's fur by picking out dirt and bugs.

primates: People, monkeys, chimpanzees, and other animals that are like them.

rank: The position a person or animal has in a group.

termites: Bugs that live in groups and eat wood.

ticks: Bugs that attach themselves to mammals and eat blood.

Find Out More

Books

Goodall, Jane. *Chimpanzees I Love: Saving Their World and Ours*. New York: Scholastic, 2001.

Goodall, Jane. *The Chimpanzee Family Book*. New York: NorthSouth Books, 1997.

Greenberg, Dan. *Chimpanzees* (Animals Animals). New York: Marshall Cavendish, 2001.

Kalman, Bobbie, and Hadley Dyer. *Endangered Chimpanzees*. New York: Crabtree Publishing Company, 2005.

Stefoff, Rebecca. *Chimpanzees* (AnimalWays). New York: Marshall Cavendish, 2004.

Websites

The Chimpanzee and Human Communication Institute
http://www.cwu.edu/~cwuchci

Friends of Washoe
http://www.friendsofwashoe.org

The Jane Goodall Institute
http://www.janegoodall.org

National Geographic Kids
http://www.kids.nationalgeographic.com/Animals/CreatureFeature/Chimpanzee

Save the Chimps.org Kids' Page
http://www.savethechimps.org/index_kids.asp

Index

Page numbers for photographs and illustrations are in **boldface**.

Africa, 18, **18**, 19, 20
arms, **4**, 6, **7**, 8

baby chimps, **9**, 14, **14**, 15, 21
birth, 14, 15
bonobos, 18, **18**, 19, **19**
brain, 8

community, **10**, 11, 13–15

fingers, 6, **7**, 8
food, 8, 12, 15, 17
foot, 6, **7**
forests, **16**, 17–19
Fouts, Roger and Deborah, **21**

Goodall, Jane, 20, **20**
grooming, 13, **13**

hand, 6, **7**

leader, 11, **12**, 15
legs, **4**, 7, **7**

mother, 13, 14, 15, 21

people, 5–8, 14, 18–21
primates, 6

rain forests, 17

sign language, 21
sleep, 13

thumb, 6, **7**
toes, 6, **7**
tools, **8**, 8–9, 20

Washoe, 21, **21**
Washington State, **21**

24

J 599.885 GRE
Greenberg, Daniel A.
Chimpanzees

ELK